Ignore
The
Impossible

Brian Reaves

Cover photos by Samuel Zeller and Mike Newbry
Cover design by Seventeen17Creative.com

DEDICATION

To my wife Lisettet, who never doubts any crazy thing I try and is always at every show cheering me on, no matter how many times she's seen the tricks done.

To my sons, Khristian and Chase, who pushed me to be the best man I could because I knew they were watching. I hope I made you proud.

CONTENTS

ACKNOWLEDGMENTS

This book came to fruition because of the exhaustive work that went into my speech for TEDxBirmingham 2017. Matthew Hamilton, Rebecca Dobrinski, and Katie Burton pushed me further than I'd imagined possible to craft the best talk I could have ever written. But like any good movie, a lot of cool footage got left on the cutting room floor. Consider this book the "Director's Cut" of my talk. Thank you, Matthew, Rebecca, and Katie. You helped me check two more things off my bucket list with the TEDx Birmingham talk and with this book.

I also want to thank my fellow magicians in the International Brotherhood of Magicians Ring 35 in Birmingham, Alabama. They are a constant source of inspiration and help keep my magic spark alive.

Thanks also my parents, Wayne and Katie Reaves, who gave me the opportunity to explore the magical possibilities in my life well after most parents would have walked away.

And finally, thanks to my son Khris for another amazing book cover and suggestions to improve the text layout of the interior.

"You need to aim beyond what you are capable of. You must develop a complete disregard for where your abilities end. Try to do things that you're incapable of... If you think you're incapable of running a company, make that your aim... Make your vision of where you want to be a reality. Nothing is impossible." - *Paul Arden*

"When facing a difficult task, act as though it is impossible to fail. If you are going after Moby Dick, take along the tartar sauce." - *H. Jackson Brown, Jr.*

"Impossible is not a fact, it's an opinion. Impossible is not a declaration, it's a dare. Impossible is potential." – *Muhammad Ali*

Brian Reaves

IGNORE THE
IMPOSSIBLE

SOLVING PROBLEMS WITH A MAGICIAN'S MINDSET

Brian Reaves

It is the opening moments of TEDx Birmingham 2017. My name is announced, and I walk out onto the stage toward the red circular piece of carpet in the spotlight. I am carrying nothing except the items in my jacket pockets, and I know what I am about to do will be streaming live over the internet and archived there for future generations. If I mess up now, this won't be something I shrug off and forget—it will be career suicide. I will become some viral video that never goes away.

The road to this point has been long and hard. It was a dream years in the making. I know if I can pull it off, I will have something checked off my bucket list that I never thought possible.

I step into the spotlight, extract a deck of cards from my jacket pocket, and smile as I prepare to create an impossible moment for the hundreds of people in attendance and the multitude watching online at that moment.

I am a magician. I live for the impossible moments in life.

THE IMPOSSIBLE MAN

"I am often dishonest in my techniques...I happily admit to cheating; it's all part of the game. I hope some of the fun for the viewer comes from not knowing what's real and what isn't." – *Derren Brown*

In July 1914, a small theater in New York City was packed with people who sat in rapt attention staring at the little man on the stage. He had promised them a miracle, and they believed he would deliver.

That man was Harry Houdini, and he had a

reputation for miracles.

As the audience watched, Harry had a huge carpet spread across the stage, effectively destroying the possibility of using a trapdoor in what he was about to do. Local bricklayers came forward and began to meticulously lay brick one on top of the other down the center of the stage. The final result was a wall roughly ten feet high by twelve feet wide.

When they finished, audience members were brought on stage to inspect the wall and the floor, and then to circle the wall so it could be seen on all sides. A frame with curtains on it was brought forward and set on one side of the wall. A similar frame was set on the other.

From the New York World

THE BRICK WALL TRICK

In full view of the audience, surrounded by people, Harry said, "I am going," and stepped into the wooden frame on one side of the wall. A few seconds later, he stepped out of the other frame on the other side of the brick wall and said, "I am here now."

There was dead silence in the room for almost two minutes before the audience finally collected themselves enough to begin applauding the miracle they had just seen.

And Harry Houdini became known as "the man

who walked through walls."

So, here's my question to you to start things off: How did he do it?

Over the years, people have come up with some pretty incredible explanations, but let me cross a few things off your list:

- The wall truthfully was solid.
- The carpet on the floor covered the stage and was also solid with no slits in it.
- The frame extended to his height and a little wider, but the edges and top of the wall could easily be seen by the audience surrounding it.
- The men who built the walls were professionals, not magicians or assistants. They were not "in on it" and had no instructions to do anything questionable.

Got it figured out? I've heard everything from Houdini having a twin to alien abductions, and the funny thing is how difficult everyone makes it. A German booklet was even published with detailed explanations for the trick involving, among other things, mechanical arms and crowd control—all of which were wrong. A simple solution is out there, but we automatically drift to the most intricate things possible.

In life, we all face problems at one time or another. It can be something as simple as having a flat tire to a more difficult thing of trying to start a business. Sometimes solutions are easy to find, while other times they seem almost impossible.

Most people you meet have a naturally negative slant in their thinking that they have to overcome. Maybe it's the constant onslaught of bad news from the television or internet (after all, bad news sells papers,

> *Most people have a naturally negative slant in their thinking that they have to overcome.*

so they say). Maybe it's just a gradual pile-up of negative moments in life that finally overshadows the good we see. But whatever the reason, it happens to just about everyone.

Unfortunately, that means that we are already unsteady in our thinking long before a problem or opportunity come our way. When it does show up, it catches us reeling and can send us sprawling because we are trying to find the solution to our now "impossible" problem.

But is it really "impossible"? As Inigo Montoya says in *The Princess Bride*: "I do not think that word means what you think it means."

In this book, I am not going to hypnotize you or offer you some deep meditation on a mountaintop somewhere to become one with the universe. If we meet in person, I will always be willing to show you some sleight of hand magic trick that just might make you a believer in magic, yet in this book, I won't be pulling anything from my sleeves. I am a magician, but you won't have to take some oath of secrecy for what you're about to learn. It's all just going to take a few minor—or major—adjustments in your thinking.

We will get back to Houdini's wall later. I promise to give you the answer to how he did it in a later chapter as we compare it to your theory. For now, I want you to consider your "impossible problem." Thinking about it ahead of time will give you a reference point for the rest of this book. Right now, it may seem insurmountable, and I get that.

As we discuss what lies ahead through the miracles of others, I hope you find that spark that lets you see another angle and changes the outcome in your life.

Along the way, we are going to look at the success stories of others who faced problems of their own. And to finish things off, I'm going to give you the opportunity to see what it's like to create magic in the lives of others by teaching you an illusion that you can do.

Who knows? You may enjoy it enough to drop what you're doing and start a career in magic!

What I can't do is solve your problem for you. And I'm not going to sit here and say, "Your problem is minor; just get over it and move on." The solutions in this book are not for every situation.

But statistically speaking, I feel safe in saying this should work for many of the problems someone reading this book might face. Not all, and not in every situation, but many of them.

This isn't a cop-out; it is me being respectful to

you and your individual situation. Aspirin helps a headache, but it doesn't cure cancer. Likewise, I hope this book helps you focus on and tackle your problem. And I hope this may take some of the intimidation out of the problem you are facing.

Get ready to dive into the way a magician's mind works...

Response Time:

What are three problems you are facing right now?

_____

_____

_____

_____

Which would you consider "impossible" and is going to be your focus as you read this book?

_____

_____

_____

If you could change one thing about yourself right now, what would it be?

_____

_____

_____

_____

WHAT IS "IMPOSSIBLE"?

"As a magician, I think everything is possible. And I think if something is done by one person it can be done by others." — *David Blaine*

I have a banner that I put up in some of my shows with a quote from Walt Disney: "It's kind of fun to do the impossible."

If anyone should know, it's Disney. He brought things to life on the screen that other people could have never imagined possible. He was the first one to pioneer a feature-length animated movie with *Snow White and the Seven Dwarves,* even though he was told time and again that people wouldn't sit through an entire movie-length cartoon. He ignored the naysayers and proved them all wrong. That movie went on to win an honorary Academy Award for what it accomplished, while Walt went on to win over thirty Academy Awards in his lifetime.

Eventually, he gave us animated movies like *Peter Pan, Robin Hood, Dumbo,* and others that we enjoyed as children and raised our own children with as well.

Then he decided to create the greatest theme park the world had ever seen in Disneyland. And he continued to improve on everything up until his death. Whatever he imagined, he tried to find a way to bring it to reality.

But that's just the good stuff. Most folks never think about the things Disney did wrong or bad things that happened to him.

In 1919, Disney was fired by the editor from his job at the Kansas City Star paper because he "lacked imagination and had no good ideas."

Walt's first major cartoon character was called "Oswald, the Lucky Rabbit." Walt had big plans and thought Oswald was his ticket until he lost the rights to his creation in a legal battle. He decided to move to Hollywood, and along the way, he dreamed up a new character. This one would be a mouse.

Today, Mickey Mouse is a household name while Oswald the Lucky Rabbit hasn't been so lucky and has faded into obscurity.

Disney had his animation studio confiscated by the government during World War Two for a temporary base. He had to have a government I.D. just to get into his own building! But instead of quitting or giving up during that time, he created a cartoon short starring Donald Duck to try and encourage Americans to pay their taxes even though they weren't legally required to at the time (imagine how wonderful life would be if that were still just a suggestion). Those monies paid in taxes served to help win the war.

Walt lived in terror that his daughters would be kidnapped like the Charles Lindbergh baby, so he and his wife stayed home with them nightly rather than live the Hollywood high life. He allowed his fear to cause him to miss out on rubbing elbows with the elite, but the valuable family time allowed him to keep a close relationship with his children.

He suffered a number of nervous breakdowns over the course of his life. Many times, he questioned his ability to succeed in animation.

His second honeymoon with his wife led to him traveling all the way across the U.S. to take a relaxing river cruise, only to find that it had to be canceled due to the Great Depression.

> *"Quitters never make it past the first failure, while winners keep failing until they succeed."*

You need to understand something: Disney did the seemingly "impossible"— but none of it came easily. Every setback just caused him to focus on a new way to accomplish whatever he was envisioning at the time.

I heard someone say, "Quitters never make it past the first failure, while winners keep failing until they succeed."

"Impossible" is our default sometimes when the task really isn't impossible, just difficult. Too many times we give up on something because it will require a little extra effort and we just say it can't be done.

If we believe in ourselves and our abilities, we can accomplish almost anything—even things other people would deem "impossible."

Since 1918, Nathan's Hot Dogs has held an annual hot dog eating competition. Up until 2000, the world record was twenty-five hot dogs in twelve minutes. It seemed like a fairly safe record that would be hard to break. Imagine eating a hot dog in approximately thirty seconds...it's going to be uncomfortable but doable.

But then in 2001, a man named Takeru Kobayashi entered the competition. He not only broke the record, but he also annihilated it. He downed *fifty* hot dogs in twelve minutes, and suddenly the bar was raised everywhere. You have to imagine eating a hot dog in about *fifteen seconds.* Go ahead; look at that on your watch and think about what that would entail.

Kobayashi would go on to win that competition for six consecutive years. He even broke his previous record by going to *fifty-three* hot dogs, and since Kobayashi broke that fifty mark, five other men have done the same in that annual event, with the current record as of this writing at *seventy* hot dogs in *ten* minutes (*two fewer minutes* than before but with *twenty* more eaten!).

For anyone keeping score, that would be like eating one every eight-and-a-half seconds. And if you're interested, you can watch these competitions on the internet. Just be warned that not everyone can keep up and sometimes the food fights back for some of the competitors.

Now, did something happen to people's stomachs in 2001 that suddenly allowed them to hold more food? Or is it safer to assume that something changed in the mindsets of those competitive eaters that said twenty-five wasn't a record set in stone?

They changed their mindset and suddenly shattered world records.

Perhaps the more familiar story for you involves Roger Bannister, who in 1954 became the first man to break the four-minute mile mark, even though medical professionals thought it would be terminal for a human body to go that fast.

After Roger broke that seemingly insurmountable goal, other people followed suit and now over 1,400 athletes have beaten that time. As of this writing, the current record stands at just over three minutes and forty-five seconds. Over a thousand athletes have proven the medical professionals of those early days incorrect.

Nelson Mandela said, "It always seems impossible until it's done." That's been true quite often in history.

You've heard people tell you to think "outside the box", but that statement implies you are in a box already and have these limitations on you. I'm saying never allow yourself to be put in the box in the first place.

Granted, sometimes we are forced to have limits on us in certain situations, but it doesn't happen every time. How many times do we put the limits on ourselves before we even begin?

So many people try to do things and give up in

frustration because they underestimated the work involved. They see the goal, they see where they are starting from, and can't find a way to reach that finish line so they give up in frustration.

But as a magician, we have to start with the goal and work our way back. Again, if it's not "impossible", it's not magic. So, if the objective is to make an elephant disappear on stage, we know ahead of time it's not naturally going to do it, but we work backward from that intended aim to figure out how to make it happen.

"Impossible" is our default sometimes when the task isn't really impossible, just difficult. Too many times we give up on something because it will require a little extra effort and we just say it can't be done.

That's an example of the roundabout thinking we are going to be putting into practice later in this book.

But why am I coming at all this from a magic slant? What makes a magician a problem-solver?

I think it's because we are forced to create miracles no one else has to consider. I know each profession has their own unique slant on problem-solving, but magicians are one of the few that don't always base their answers on real-world limitations.

Let me tell you how I got introduced to this method of thinking and how I got started in magic. It was a single moment a little over twenty-five years ago that changed my life forever.

I was managing a quick-service restaurant at the time and it was a slow afternoon. One of the kids working that day pulled out a deck of cards and said, "Pick a card."

That little phrase honestly set my life in a totally different direction.

I chose a card, and he proceeded to find it in various incredible ways. He shuffled it and found it. He showed me cards that I knew weren't mine, and yet magically one was. Somehow, *I found my own card* by picking a random one.

I had never seen anything like it up close. I had

watched magicians on television and grew up never missing those David Copperfield specials every year—but this was happening *to me* right in front of me.

I was a part of the magic.

It was a feeling I never forgot, and it was a sensation I wanted to replicate in the lives of others. For a few brief seconds, reality seemed to bend for me.

That moment—that *feeling* where for just an instant anything was possible—was the exact moment I decided to become a magician. It was a time where I saw something take place that couldn't possibly happen. I realized my way of thinking had been all wrong up to that point.

But the art of magic is the art of subterfuge. What you think you see isn't always what you see. There are things going on you probably never notice. That's why it's called "misdirection".

When I got off work after seeing that first card trick, I dug out a deck of cards at my house and tried the things I'd seen.

They didn't work for me.

I drove thirty minutes to the closest bookstore and bought the only magic book they had (I still have it, and I still regularly perform tricks from it). I found out there were moves he'd been doing I'd never noticed.

And that's what had fooled me. I had imagined every card he dealt as the card it should have been. I'd never realized he was slipping a card back or dealing a different card from the one I had seen.

In other words, it never dawned on me that you could cheat. Magic tricks don't play by the rules. The thinking isn't linear, it's circular. When you want to devise a magical miracle, you have to approach it in a very creative way.

As I got involved in the art of illusion and how magicians think, I noticed my way of thinking started to change in other areas too. Rather than come at things in a direct, straight-to-the-point method, I started to incorporate some of the roundabout thinking involved in creating a magic trick.

It opened my eyes to an entirely new way of

problem-solving. And I hadn't even realized I was stuck in a rut until I found there was an alternative.

I didn't cheat in my decision-making. Instead, I began to realize that just because we needed something to happen as an end result didn't mean the only way to make it happen was to go straight from A to B. You could very creatively reach that same result by jumping to D, then J, then take a slight right at S, touch briefly on W, before landing at B. Seems incredibly con-voluted, I know, but when you can't find a solution to a problem sometimes the best thing you can do is start stretching your thinking.

Let's go back to the scenario of making an elephant disappear on stage. There are several ways to do that.

- ✓ You could turn the elephant invisible.

- ✓ You could push it into a wormhole in time and space and teleport it to another dimension.

- ✓ You could fill it with helium and have it float above the crowd while they were still watching the stage.

✓ You could give it a "magic" feather and let it fly out of there (hey, it worked for Dumbo).

But since none of those things are feasible to normal human beings, you'd need to get creative.

That's where the term "smoke and mirrors" comes in to play.

With a little cheating, a little creativity, a lot of misdirection, and more careful choreography of people, places, and a pachyderm than you could ever imagine, that big gray beauty will be seen one second and be gone when the curtain falls the next.

> *Not every starting point is in view of the finish line.*

But it requires a change in your thinking—a *serious* change in your thinking.

We are raised to understand that the shortest distance between two points is a straight line. But what if you can't reach those two points in a straight line? What if there is a barrier between point "A" and "B"?

That's what you are going to have to consider as we go forward in this book. Not every distance is surmountable with a straight run, and not every starting point is in view of the finish line.

Response Time:

Have you ever thought something couldn't be done, only to see someone else do it later? If so, what was it?

_____

_____

_____

_____

_____

Be completely honest with yourself: Looking at the "impossible" problem in your life from chapter 1, is it possible the problem isn't so much "impossible" as it is just "difficult"? Is there something you could do that might require extra effort but would help you find the answer?

_____

_____

_____

_____

_____

"Magic is believing in yourself. If you can do that, you can make anything happen."
– *Johann Wolfgang von Goethe*

A MAGICIAN'S VIEWPOINT

"My brain is the key that sets me free." – *Harry Houdini*

I'm going to let you in on a little secret about being a magician: you and I see the world differently.

In actuality, the world for both of us is the same. I don't see spirits floating around the room or cartoon character animals singing a Disney tune and alighting on people's shoulders. The medication has taken care of all that.

No, I'm saying the way we *look at things* is

different. And I'm not alone in my opinion.

According to a recent article in *New Scientist* magazine ("Creative People Physically See and Process the World Differently", *New Scientist*, April 22, 2017), people who are open to new experiences actually *do* see the world differently from the rest. They do well at tests where they try to find new and creative uses for everyday objects like bricks, mugs, or table tennis balls (all of which I have used in some form or another in magic tricks).

"Their brains are able to flexibly engage with less conventional solutions," lead author Anna Antinori, a psychologist at the University of Melbourne in Australia, told *New Scientist*. "We believe this is the first empirical evidence that they have different visual experiences to the average individual."

They tested one hundred and twenty-three university students by giving them a "binocular rivalry test," which was a set of special binoculars that had a red dot in one side and a green dot in the others. Most folks saw both colors, alternating between the two, but there was a select group that actually saw the two colors merge into one multi-colored image.

Those were the creatives. Those are my people.

They weren't magicians, mind you. They were just creative folks, but I hope we can agree that you have to be pretty creative to be an illusionist. Look at the closest object to you (besides this book) and try to come up with a new use for that object. Now imagine using that object in a magic trick or maybe you've even seen someone use that object in a trick before. If you've got a new use for that item, you just might be a creative too.

That's what I mean when I say we all live in the same world but see it differently in a lot of respects.

For example, when you pull out a pocket full of change, you look at the coins and try to figure out what to buy. I pull out a coin and try to figure out how to make it vanish.

You see, a coin doesn't naturally vanish unless you throw it somewhere. You don't just close your hand and open it to find the coin has disappeared. It doesn't happen.

As a matter of fact, there might be some of you reading today who would argue that a coin *can't* vanish; that it's *impossible* to close your hand and have a coin disappear. And in the natural, I would have to agree.

But I'm a magician, and as I said before, we see the world very differently.

I cannot close my hand and have a coin disappear using the normal method. But it's entirely possible if I just change the rules a little and think about it in a whole new way.

Every magician faces three types of spectators when he performs. You may not even realize you are one of these people, but by the end of the book you will probably be able to safely say which one best describes you.

With a little extra effort, I can make it happen (and a whole lot easier than the elephant scenario from the last chapter).

There is no greater satisfaction for a magician than that moment when a coin vanish is so perfect you can hear an audible response from the crowd; when the eyes are flying all around trying to find the piece of silver they just saw but that is no more.

Some effort, bending the rules just a bit and the right timing allows me to make possible what people might have considered impossible.

And that impossible feeling is what motivates and creates magicians everywhere.

But a magician can only be amazing when there is someone there to see it happen. That's where spectators come in.

Believe it or not, you have something in common with a lot of folks. In fact, I feel safe in saying I can categorize you fairly accurately in the next few pages.

Every magician faces three types of spectators when he performs. You may not even realize you are one of these people, but by the end of the book, you will probably be able to safely say which one best describes you.

At the same time, when any magician wants to create a magical miracle, he has to approach it in a very creative way. It is generally a three-phase thinking process that mirrors the three types of spectators they face when performing.

I mentioned in the last chapter that I noticed my way of thinking changed the more I got involved with the art of illusion. Now it's time to show you exactly what I mean.

Imagine we are sitting with a group of people. I pull out a deck of cards and begin to shuffle. I lean toward the person in front of me and say with a smile, "Pick a card."

The card is chosen, signed by the spectator, and shuffled back into the deck. After some byplay, I ask the spectator to stand up.

They do so, turn to look at their chair and see a face-down card. When the spectator turns the card over, it is the one they signed. They've been sitting on it the whole time—technically even *before they signed it.*

There are three reactions I will get from the crowd...

<u>Response Time</u>

Do you currently consider yourself a "creative", or do you feel your thinking is more of a linear, straight-to-the-point way of looking at things?

_____

_____

_____

What was the last major problem you faced in life that you would now consider "solved"?

_____

_____

_____

Did you have a detailed plan of how you were going to handle it, or did you just feel like you were winging it the whole time? And if you had a detailed plan ahead of time, did you actually follow that plan?

_____

_____

_____

"There is magic, but you have to be the magician. You have to make the magic happen." – *Sidney Sheldon*

"I think magic is very related to happiness. So it is not there all the time, but there are moments of magic in everyone's life." – *Penelope Cruz*

THE FIRST TYPE OF SPECTATOR

"Everybody wants to change, but nobody wants to do anything differently." – *Eugene Burger*

The first type of spectator is the one who says **"That's impossible! It can't be done!"** and shuts it down. That's it, go home, we are finished here. The suggested goal is beyond their belief system, and therefore they give up before it even begins.

This happens about fifty percent of the time for me. Someone will throw up their hands, scream something, and walk away saying, "No way, nope, that didn't happen." Usually, they will come back to see another trick, but they aren't even *trying* to figure it out. They are enjoying the magic—which I appreciate—but the entire concept of how it's done is too much for them to want to try to comprehend.

Notice I'm not saying they *can't* comprehend it. The trickery is surprising simple to follow most of the time. It would just require more effort than they are willing to invest in the situation.

Unfortunately, this can translate to life as well with people giving up way too soon on things before really just putting in a little effort to see it through.

It's important that we tackle this first and get it out of the way: *If you are this type of spectator, you have the most work ahead of you—but it's a rewarding journey.*

Not every answer is easy. Not every solution will be found on the first try. Sometimes the solution won't be found until well after most folks will have thrown up their hands in frustration and given up.

Dale Carnegie said, "Most of the important things in the world have been accomplished by people who have kept on trying when there seemed to be no hope at all."

If you are the kind of person who sees the problem, looks around for the solution, and not finding one says, "It can't be done," you are who I am describing.

But the most important thing to remember is that you *can* change to the "extra effort" kind of person. You don't have to stay the way you are if you don't want to.

And I'm not saying you're wrong if you are this type of person; I'd just like to challenge you to a new way of thinking.

I mentioned earlier the three phases of thinking a magician has to consider when wanting to create a magic effect. This first type of spectator says "It can't be done," but as a magician, the first step I have to take when wanting to create a magical miracle is to **approach it with an open mind**. I cannot say it can't be done. I have to say it can be done *when*—not *if*—I find the solution.

See, some tasks truly are insurmountable if we keep our old way of thinking. It's when we approach them from a new direction and new perspective that we often find it's not the *task* that must change, but our *approach*.

Some people consider a problem the same way every time: head on. They are very linear thinkers and just keep chipping away until they either solve the problem or give up completely. They do not move on to B until A is solved, and they don't consider C at all until they reach that point.

Other people will circle the problem, look at it from all sides, and try to find the way that will provide a solution in the quickest time possible. Sometimes they will even stretch the people around them because their approach is so unorthodox to what many people consider the norm.

Let me give you an example of how this can work in your own life. Take a look at this set of letters:

OMLMD   IHFYT   ALALT   ATGBSS
ATCDSM AYSM INYL INYL GSYL TM

How long would it take you to memorize that set of letters in that order? Study it carefully and think about it. What do you think? Maybe an hour? Maybe a couple of hours? Some of you might even be thinking you couldn't do it in a day.

A few of you might have already given up. That's too bad.

Because what if I told you that probably 90% of you will have that sequence memorized two minutes from now? In one-hundred and twenty seconds, most of you will be able to write those letters out in perfect order.

You see, the first spectator says, "It can't be done" and shuts it all down when all you have to do is change your way of looking at it just a little.

OMLMD IHFYT ALALT ATGBSS ATCDSM AYSM INYL INYL GSYL TM

Look at those letters again, and now sing this little tune: "Oh, my love, my darling, I hunger for your touch, a long, and lonely time…"

See, now some of you my age are thinking of Patrick Swayze and Demi Moore and pottery. Some of the younger folks are thinking "Who are Patrick Swayze and Demi Moore?"

But if you've heard the song "Unchained Melody" you could now write out that sequence of letters perfectly, with very little effort. And it all happened because you took off your limitations of "It can't be done" and just saw it a little differently now as "It can't be done *that* way, but it *can* be done *this* way."

Think about it for just a second: ***You basically just did something you had considered impossible a few minutes ago at first glance.***

You completed a task you didn't think you'd be able to do *in a day*, and you did it in just a *matter of seconds.*

I understand that memorizing those letters didn't have some major impact on your life. You didn't win the lottery or discover some incredible new invention that changes the world forever. But imagine if this was something that was truly important to you or your company. Imagine if this was a task that was vital to the success of your department.

We didn't do anything crazy here. I didn't hypnotize you or cast some mystical spell on any of you. You just changed your perception of the problem, and it went from "impossible" to "easy". You thought about it in a different way, and it made all the difference.

As I mentioned earlier, "impossible" is our default sometimes when the task isn't impossible, just difficult. Too many times we give up on something because it will require a little extra effort and we just say it can't be done.

Unfortunately, success requires effort almost one-hundred percent of the time.

It all becomes an endurance test. Who will give up first: you or the problem?

There is a quote by Jim Rohn that says, "How long should you try? Until."

Until what? Until you have a resolution. Until you have found a workable answer. Until you have found a positive alternative.

Until you walk away wiping the dust off your hands and saying, "That's done. What's next?".

JK Rowling was rejected by all 12 major publishers with her first *Harry Potter* book. She seemed doomed to fail until a tiny little publishing house bought it for a meager advance and published a thousand copies of it—half of which were sent to libraries.

Stephen King had his first novel, *Carrie*, rejected thirty times. At one point he threw the entire manuscript into the trash, and it was only rescued by his wife who refused to give up on his dream of writing.

> *It all becomes an endurance test. Who will give up first: you or the problem?*

Both authors faced tremendous opposition at the beginning of their careers, and both almost gave up—or *did* give up—several times. In the end, however, they both became insanely rich and successful because they pushed on to that next possible rejection or acceptance. Rowling has sold over 400 million copies of her books, and King has sold over 350 million copies of his.

I have heard that the average number of times a person tries something before quitting is *less than one*. In other words, many times they won't even try *once* if they think they might fail. How sad!

Jack Canfield said, "Don't worry about failures, worry about the chances you miss when you don't even try."

You are going to have problems in your business. Stressful things are going to come up from time to time because that's just life. But what you can do is change the way you are thinking about them. Find a new way to do it.

Understand, that's how a magician *has* to think. We have to look at something that's impossible and find a way to make it work. The impossible problem is our workshop. After all, if *anyone* can do it, it's not really magic, is it?

If I move from one side of the stage to the other, that's not magic because you can see what I'm doing and most of you could do this yourself. But if I disappear in a puff of smoke and suddenly show up over *on the other side of the room*, that's magic! And as a magician, I just have to figure out how to make that happen.

We all face problems, and some of them may indeed seem impossible. And sometimes our natural instinct may be to give up and say "That's just going to be too hard to fix. I can't do it." And maybe the problem *is* impossible if you keep looking at it the way you always have.

> *"Don't worry about failures, worry about the chances you miss when you don't even try" – Jack Canfield*

Maybe your boss wants some seemingly unattainable goal for your company this year. Maybe you are trying to set a budget and get out of debt. Maybe you are trying to find a way to mend a broken relationship or achieve some personal goal of a marathon, or writing a book, or playing a musical instrument that doesn't seem possible.

But that is a self-imposed limitation. That is thinking about the problem the way a normal person might think about them. That is seeing the desired end result with no idea of how to get there.

Simply by removing the "It can't be done" rule and looking at it another way, it is entirely possible that we can accomplish it.

Don't give up too soon just because the first glance at the problem doesn't yield an immediate answer.

Getting to the finish line is going to require perseverance. If you are this type of spectator, fight the urge to give up without an easy answer and make a personal commitment that you will begin to search for a solution even though it doesn't seem obvious.

<u>Step 1:</u>

Approach the problem with an open mind. It can be done when—not if—you find the solution.

<u>Response Time</u>

Is there a problem in your past that comes to mind when you consider a time when you might have given up too easily?

_____

_____

_____

_____

When you finally solved that problem, was the answer something much easier than you considered before?

_____

_____

_____

What do you need to change about the way you approach a problem?

_____

_____

_____

_____

"Without the work, the magic won't come."
– *Jay Z*

"So much magic lies beyond our fears."
- *Kathryn Budig*

THE SECOND TYPE OF SPECTATOR

"Sometimes magic is just someone spending more time on something than anyone else might reasonably expect."
– *Teller*

While the first spectator doesn't initially like to entertain the possibility of a solution (but we're working on that, right?), the second spectator says **"That's impossible. I wonder how *he* did that?"**

This happens about forty-five percent of the time for me. Someone will say, "How did you do that?" And the *particularly* ambitious ones will say, "Can you teach *me* how to do that?"

That's good because that means that even though you acknowledge the end result is impossible, you know *it was done* and just want to know how. These are the types of leaders who say, "Let's reach this goal through the established path someone else took."

That's the second step I have to take when approaching the magic miracle: **I ask "What has worked for others in the past to accomplish this goal?"**

I recently attended a leadership conference by a man who leads a multi-site organization of over thirty-thousand people. He takes one or two days a week off, and his organization is thriving simply because he has developed a staff capable of running the little things while he takes care of the big ones.

On the other hand, I met a man there named Chuck who has a single-site organization of a few hundred that will not allow it to reach its full potential out of fear and weak management skills.

Both men have the same types of job, and both men have the same options available to them. One of them develops the leaders in his organization and trusts them to lead. The other doesn't have the self-confidence to raise up leaders because he's afraid they'll challenge his ideas and he won't be able to defend his decisions.

Unfortunately, Chuck is holding back *his entire organization* simply because his ambition is crippled by insecurity. That means one man is hindering an entire team of potential leaders in spite of the obvious answers available.

Both men are completely capable of running huge companies, yet the one who says "It can't be done" is limiting himself to failure. Success and the path to it are laid out before him by simply following in the footsteps of the successful leader.

Many of the hard lessons have already been learned if we are willing to study what others have done in the past and develop new ideas based on their decisions.

In the last chapter, we looked at that string of letters and found a quick and easy way to memorize them. What we just did was inspired by something another magician did to help me memorize something several months ago. It worked for me then, and it ultimately just worked for us.

Magic is rich with history, famous magicians who did things no one could believe. And for the student willing to put in the time and effort in research, most of the answers are out there to find. It's incredibly easy to become a clone of someone else.

If you don't believe me, go to YouTube and look up "ambitious card trick." You'll find some pretty amazing ones, but you'll also find a lot of people performing the same one. Sometimes they are better than the original. Most of the time, they are just the same or worse.

And in life, it's unfortunately easy to just become a sponge, soaking up the knowledge of others and never actually using it to do anything. Or just playing it safe and following in the footsteps of others.

Brilliant people have made incredible discoveries that deserve careful study. And yes, there's nothing wrong with that if that's who you're satisfied with being.

Honestly, who wants to do more work than you have to in pursuit of an answer to the "impossible" problem? If you can find a resolution to the problem in three steps, why on earth would you purposefully take ten?

Believe it or not, there *are* times when that's a valid choice, but that is something we'll cover when talking about that last type of spectator in the next chapter.

So, what is the problem with being this type of spectator? What's wrong with going through the established methods of others? It is a wise choice, and I can only think of one strong reason to grow beyond this step.

It kills originality.

One of the traps for magicians (and just about any other performer) is learning routines from videos instead of books. Magic books are vague in the details of some tricks, meaning the magician has to experiment to find exactly what move they are trying to describe. They often give little to no scripting, so you have a lot of moves and a great effect, but the true success of the trick lies in the individual performer's ability to entertain.

Videos are completely different. It becomes tempting to do a magic trick exactly the way you watched it being done—including the jokes the magician told. Unfortunately, this doesn't birth personal creativity; it stifles it. Instead of doing their own thinking and crafting, the lazy magician simply copies the successful routine of someone else.

The same can be said for comedians, singers, jugglers, and just about any other entertainer. You see someone become a hit doing something and you want to emulate it because you feel it's a guaranteed success.

Eddie Murphy used to tell the story of how one

of his first standup comedy routines was called "A Tribute to Richard Pryor". It wasn't really so much a tribute as it was actually just him doing some of Richard's material verbatim because he hadn't created enough of his own. Of course, Eddie grew as a comedian and eventually wrote his own jokes but imagine if he'd just kept on doing Pryor's material. We wouldn't know who he was today any more than we do some Elvis impersonator.

And if you realize this is the type of spectator you are, I challenge you to force yourself to grow. Study the successful decisions of others, but don't be afraid to forge your own path. You already have the initiative to create forward momentum in your situation; now it's just a matter of harnessing that to the next level.

The major problem with this type of spectator comes from the fact that they can occasionally get stuck in "research mode" and find so many different alternatives to reaching their goal they never even start. They can get overwhelmed by information.

Remember, there are a million possible answers

out there sometimes. So many choices can cause a brain freeze. We are so overwhelmed with possible remedies that it forces us into inaction for fear of doing the wrong thing.

Or even worse, we overthink things to the point of making bad choices. The obvious choice and answer are there, but we look at so many options we let logic jump out the window and make unwise decisions because it worked for someone else we respect.

But there are a lot of things that are so specific to one person that we cannot hope to replicate it perfectly. We have to study it, appreciate the thought and effort that went into it, and then find our own way.

For example, I would love to perform the huge illusion David Copperfield did when he made the Statue of Liberty disappear. I can research exactly how he did it (and I have) and then I can decide I'm going to try to do it the same way.

I will fail.

Why? Simply because he has a ton of money and incredibly talented staff and technicians at his disposal. I don't.

This means I can fly out to New York, take the ferry to Liberty Island, throw on some cool outfit with the wind hitting my hair just perfect, and make the magic gestures.

And nothing will happen.

Instead, I perform my own version of the "Disappearance of the Statue of Liberty" illusion—a three-inch-tall version—and I make it disappear. I admire what David did to make his illusion happen, and I even mention the fact he did it to honor him for his accomplishment— but I end up using ideas from other magic books to help form my own routine.

Find someone you can respect and be receptive to for advice that has been through a similar situation. Ask them for ideas on your specific problem. If they are truly familiar with you, that's even better because they know what can play to your strengths and weaknesses.

I know a business leader named Frank who was mentored by a very successful older man in the same field. Careful, specific-to-his-situation advice and directions were given by the mentor, and Frank took his advice for years and geared everything toward that goal.

Then he got around other, younger leaders in his field and began to see how successful they were by using other methods. Forsaking the wisdom of someone who knew him, Frank tossed out the advice of the seasoned, successful mentor to model himself after the younger guys in his field.

> *Don't get stuck in neutral unable to make a choice because you're overwhelmed by possibilities.*

The problem was that those younger guys were dynamic personalities who knew how to motivate people to work for and with them. Frank wasn't anything like that.

But again, he let the overflow of information into his life cause him to second-guess good advice and guidance, and as a result, there were some horrible decisions made in his organization. The direction of things went way off-base from where the team had been headed, and the only good reason given was because Frank changed his mind.

Unfortunately, Frank had spent so much time selling his team on their original direction for the company that they had bought into it wholeheartedly (which is exactly what you want in normal circumstances). When he suddenly decided to change directions, he had to rationalize it without obvious advantages over their original direction. His team ended up meandering in confusion with a lack of real motivation.

Get input from the people who know you. Talk to them about ideas you are toying with to solve your problem and give them specific examples of how others in the past solved similar problems and why you are considering that for your situation. Then make a decision and lead your team to the solution.

The only time you should change direction mid-stride is when you are willing to acknowledge to your team that you made a mistake.

And for goodness sake, don't be one of those

people who say, "I never make mistakes. I create learning opportunities." Suck it up and admit you made the wrong call. I promise you that everyone else knows you did. Being able to own your blunders shows leadership potential and self-confidence. On the other hand, trying to dance around your gaffes and act like they never happened fools no one and makes you seem very insecure. People follow leaders they trust and respect, and when that respect is lost, it is hard to regain.

You have to be educated and well-informed to make the best decisions possible. Look at what others did in the past to accomplish the goal. Carefully consider all options. But don't get stuck in neutral unable to make a choice because you're overwhelmed by possibilities.

If you are this type of spectator, you are ready to resolve the situation you face. You are most likely prepared to do whatever it takes to fix it. You have the determination to see it through, but you lack the fortitude to craft your own solution. Make a personal commitment now to change that and focus your momentum toward an answer with your own twist on it.

Some people say "There's no need to reinvent the wheel," but that doesn't work for the final type of spectator.

<u>Step 2:</u>

Look at what has worked for others in the past to accomplish a similar goal.

Will their solution—or a variation of it— work for you?

Response Time

Do some research before answering this one.
Have you ever heard about someone facing a
problem similar to your own? What was it?

_____

_____

_____

_____

How did they solve that problem?

_____

_____

_____

_____

What did they do that you could possibly adapt
to your situation? Is there something they did
that you haven't considered before?

_____

_____

_____

_____

THE THIRD TYPE OF SPECTATOR

"Practice until it becomes boring. Then practice until it becomes beautiful." – *Harry Blackstone, Jr.*

So, the first spectator shuts it down and doesn't try. The second spectator admits it can be done but doesn't see a need to blaze their own path.

But here comes the third spectator!

The third spectator is the one who says **"That's impossible. I wonder how *I* could do that?"** And that's the one! That's the one who says "I thought it couldn't be done, but it *was*. Now that goal is shattered so how can I make it happen too?". That's the mindset of a magician in the making. It's the mentality of someone who is ready to blow past their preconceived limitations and create a miracle.

They don't want to follow in someone else's footsteps. They want to figure it out themselves. They are the ones who have finally captured that thinking that says, "It's possible! I don't know *how* yet, but I know it *can* be done! I just need to figure it all out to make it happen!"

This happens about five percent of the time for me. It takes effort to replicate the success of others in your own way. Originality requires intention.

That's where I have to go in my third step to create a magic miracle: **I have to ask "How am I uniquely gifted to solve this problem? What knowledge do I have that I can combine with my own little quirks, inspirations, and ideas to make this happen?"**

And that is the mindset of a magician. That is also the mindset of a leader who says, "I don't know how we're going to do it, but we *are* going to do it."

Going back to the Elvis impersonator analogy

from the last chapter for a moment, consider *why* there are so many of them out there. Elvis was dynamic, electric on stage, and different from everyone who had preceded him.

There are tribute shows for the Beatles, Michael Jackson, and many others. Some of them are perfect copies of the originals, even able to emulate vocal acrobatics that made the original singer unique.

But then consider this: how many incredible singers take an old song someone else has done and put their unique spin on it to create something dynamic that only *they* could do?

Dolly Parton wrote and performed a song called "I Will Always Love You", but most of us hear Whitney Houston's voice in our head when we think of it because she made that song her own. Since then, Whitney has been copied a million times in Karaoke bars across the nation, but she was the trailblazer.

A good leader can take something someone else has done and find ways to improve it. They find ways to include their own signature touch to the finished product. Maybe the original is still in there somewhere, but by the same token, you can tell something powerful has been added.

Strong leaders do that. They study the past, and then they cut loose on their own from the fire of some spark of creativity they saw in the potential of the original.

In 1996, a then-unknown magician named David Blaine had his first TV special called "Street Magic". This was before he was doing the crazy endurance stunts; he was simply doing magic tricks. David Copperfield had dropped off the television radar, and the world was ripe for more magic.

Blaine did not disappoint.

It wasn't his performing style. His insouciant attitude made him seem like he was pretty much bored throughout the show.

It wasn't some flashy setting. He truly did just do magic on the streets in various cities. There were no flashpots or pyros out there with blaring music and beautiful assistants.

It all boiled down to his magic trick choices. The people he performed for on the show were speechless at times. The viewers watching at home were hooked and loving it. David became an overnight sensation and has had several specials and a tour since then.

But here's the thing about it: David was using

tricks that most other magicians had long since tossed aside in their "magic junk drawer" as too simple or boring. He didn't really create anything in that show; he just used existing tricks and put his spin on them. He was a visionary at the time and has only improved since.

To make it easier for a non-magician to understand, imagine twenty people in an art class all being given green crayons and told to draw a picture. Consider what would happen if nineteen of those people drew grassy fields, but then one person drew a great dragon flying over a forest of trees. In essence, that's what David did. He took the tricks and threw away the instructions, creating his own.

Now David is an incredible showman with several more television specials and a tour under his belt. Instead of doing standard tricks, he's doing some unorthodox things it's safe to say no one else is trying. He kept building on that original desire to create his brand, and it has worked to make him a huge success.

Take a look at yourself. Are you that kind of leader? There is a lot of extra effort involved in taking something someone else has done and improving on it. It takes a creative spark, considerable self-confidence, and most of the time a team to really look at it from all angles and make it something special.

This type of leader isn't willing to rest on the accomplishments of others. And while it requires work, these are the types of leaders you see excel in their individual fields. They are the ones who go to bed considering new ways to accomplish their goals and wake up the next morning with new ideas and theories.

> *This type of leader isn't willing to just rest on the accomplishments of others...these are the type of leaders you see excel in their individual fields.*

This is the type of leader people want to follow. They see originality and a clear vision for the future in this type of person. This trailblazer sets goals for their team and organization and isn't afraid to set them high—but clear direction and potential proven steps are given to attain those lofty goals. It's not a "wish list" of unattainable objectives that just serve to demotivate the people who serve under them. If those goals aren't met, the director isn't afraid to accept responsibility when they made a bad decision.

This is an active role, not a passive one. It is not a position one tries to take without an inherent desire to succeed and listen to those around them.

While this is the type of leader I am pushing you toward becoming, I realize it's not for everyone. Some people just don't want to put forth that effort and put in the time to find their own way. But I challenge you to make yourself grow in that direction.

Maybe you don't think you can do it. Maybe you don't believe you're capable of more than just "average".

Well, I'm about to prove you wrong.

During my presentations when I am speaking on this topic, the next few moments are my favorite in the entire show. The reason is simple: I'm about to demonstrate how you are truly capable of much more than you ever imagined.

It's time to go back to that little theater in New York moments after Houdini walked through his brick wall and explain how it was done. I am going to describe his actual method.

But if you've been reading carefully and answering the questions at the end of each chapter, you already know the solution.

Step 3:

Look at every aspect of who you are and what makes you unique. You approach things differently from anyone else you know simply because of your own personal experiences and insights.

How are you uniquely gifted to solve this problem?

What knowledge do you already have that you can combine with your own little quirks, inspirations, and ideas to find the solution?

Response Time

When was the last time you truly did something of your own and put your own spin on something you were doing?

_____

_____

_____

Have you ever seen someone else solve a problem and think "Where did that idea come from?"? Did their solution spark you into coming up with one of your own?

_____

_____

_____

_____

What are you willing to do to solve your "impossible" problem? Give a clear answer, not "Whatever it takes".

_____

_____

_____

_____

WALKING THROUGH A BRICK WALL
(HOUDINI'S SOLUTION)

"I love amazing people. I love dazzling them. That's why I think performing magic is one of the greatest things a person can do." – *Ricky Jay*

"The mind is led on, step by step, to defeat its own logic." – *Dai Vernon*

Do you believe in yourself enough to know you can do it?

Ironically enough, my job as a magician is to make you *believe*. I know it sounds odd since magicians do so many things that you know are impossible, but that's our goal: to make you *believe* it's possible. If you hold to the fact that it's a charade, then there is no magic; there is only trickery. Our objective is to make you have that moment where you suspend your disbelief and believe in the impossible.

And that takes us back to our brick wall story in the first chapter. Have you had a chance to figure that out yet, or at least have a theory?

A quick recap of the situation and possibilities:

A brick wall was constructed on a rug in the middle of the stage by real bricklayers. The carpet was a solid piece with no slits for trapdoors or anything. The bricks were real. The wall was solid. You could easily see the top, bottom, and sides of the wall at all times, and the audience members surrounding the wall were not stooges or paid off in any way.

In full view of the audience, surrounded by people, Harry said, "I am going," and stepped into the wooden frame on one side of the wall. A few seconds later, he stepped out of the other frame on the other side of the brick wall and said, "I am here now".

Got it figured out? I promise that you currently have enough information to put it all together yourself right now. The answer is staring you in the face. Don't give up too soon.

Knowing what you know now and having read the things you've read up until this point on giving up too soon, how would *you* do it if you had to?

Before you chastise me for breaking the magician's code by telling you the answer, let me defend myself by saying you can just Google "Houdini walking through a brick wall" and get the solution immediately. I'm saving you the slight trouble of an internet search, but feel free to go that route if you are worried that rogue illusionists are going to sneak in your house and turn your pets into frogs because you have stolen a secret.

> *"We would accomplish many more things if we did not think of them as impossible." – Marcus Aurelius*

Ready for the real answer as to how Harry did it? It's simple: he used a trapdoor that opened under the wall. The rug sagged on the open door, creating a comfy little tunnel for him to slide through. When he was safely on the other side, the trap door was shut, and Harry emerged as the man who walked through walls.

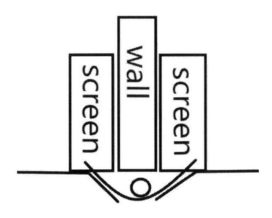

And now you think I conned you. You think I lied to you or misled you in some way with the information I gave you, but read it all again.

The odds are likely you thought early on about going under the wall, but then you immediately discounted it because of the rug. The kicker is that the rug was a vital part of the escape.

You probably considered the real solution at some point in your thinking, and then you doubted yourself and second-guessed until you gave up. You may have even heard me mention the rug and then you tossed your idea out.

A great magician named Dai Vernon once made a statement as he was describing how to do a trick. He said, "The mind is led on, step by step, to defeat its own logic." What he meant was that the spectator could figure out the effect when they saw it, but by simply adding a "convincer" or a slight twist here and there they would begin to doubt their solution to the point of completely giving up—even though they actually had figured it out early on.

And that's what I've been talking about the whole time. The solutions are there waiting for us, and so many times we hit upon a great idea that could make the impossible possible—until we overthink things and suddenly convince ourselves it's never going to work.

We talk ourselves into inaction rather than take a chance on failure.

Think about the number one hindrance to solving your impossible problem today. What is that one aspect you have the most difficulty reasoning around? Is there any possibility that hindrance could actually become an essential step toward the answer to the problem rather than an all-out stopping point?

Tony Robbins summed it up perfectly: "What we can or cannot do, what we consider possible or impossible, is rarely a function of our true capability. It is more likely a function of our beliefs about who we are."

I know so many people who have incredible ideas and unique concepts that could make them great successes in their chosen field or in another field of interest they would love to enter. You can see their eyes light up as soon as they start talking about that one idea that sets them going. But then as I issue the challenge to them to give it a shot, the light immediately goes out, and they give a hundred reasons why it would never work.

Imagine how horrible it is to watch them killing their own dreams by turning their possibilities into impossibilities.

Now, it's easy to understand why most folks have a natural tendency to do this. Truthfully, it's so much safer to say "I *could* have..." rather than to actually *try* something unsuccessfully and be forced to say "It didn't work."

I knew an incredibly talented musician and singer who was a gifted songwriter with the ability to draw you in with every song. I've sat and watched a woman break down in tears talking about how a particular song he had written resonated with her. Truthfully, this guy was a goldmine waiting to be discovered.

> *Is there any possibility that hindrance could actually become an essential step toward the answer of the problem rather than an all-out stopping point?*

But then if you asked him about performing or the newest song he'd written, you could see his self-confidence falter a little.

I can't write hit songs, and I wish I could. I've tried in the past, finally admitting to the fact that it's not my calling. And before you start saying, "Yeah, and here you are telling us not to give up!", I have tried and tried because it was my *desire* to write songs, but "desire" and "gifting" are two different things. And hey, I *tried*—which is more than could be said for a lot of folks.

Anyway, my friend finally entered an open mic night contest in a nearby venue. The contest was judged by the people performing that night. That means each performer got a score sheet and had to score their competition. No one had a reason to be kind, in other words.

Some of them sang originals, some of them did cover songs, and most of them were good.

Then my friend took the stage. His entire persona changed, and he completely transformed as he stepped up to the microphone. He performed two original songs and utterly captivated the crowd. It was the first real singing competition he had ever entered.

And that night he won first place.

Later they invited all the past champions back for a competition. This time my friend faced eleven other people who had won the same competition at some time or another. These were mostly all polished performances with the singers giving their everything.

And my friend won that night too.

But it would never have happened if he hadn't been willing to fail that night as well.

You have to have thick skin if you want to be a success. There are those around you who will make it their life choice to tear you down lest you make them look inferior by succeeding where they themselves have failed (or refused to try).

But you have to be willing to shut out those negative voices.

> *You could be holding on to that solution that's ready to thrust you into the spotlight. Suck it up and say, "I may fail, but if I do at least I will know one way it won't work."*

That doesn't mean you don't listen to any voices of reason altogether. You have to have people in your life you respect who know you and for whom you are willing to step back and reorganize if they are uncomfortable with a direction you are going. That's where Frank failed in our earlier example; he refused to take direction from someone with his best interest at heart.

The voices I'm talking about are the negative voices in general; the ones who don't *ever* think you can accomplish anything. Learn to tune out those who just want to tear you down all the time, but it's vitally important that we find people who can keep us grounded if we go too far.

Besides, the people who can act as the voice of reason in our lives are usually the people who *most* want you to succeed anyway. They will be there to cheer you on as you press through.

How about you? What "impossible dream" do you have in your life right now? Have you ever honestly put forth an effort to get the ball rolling to give it a fair shot?

What crazy idea do you have that would let you "walk through a brick wall"? I'm speaking figuratively, of course—unless you actually do have an idea on how to do that in which case yay for you!

What inspiration do you have for your company that you think would make money if you just dared to take it to your boss? Have you talked yourself out of it because the thinking behind it is radical and doesn't seem like it could possibly work? Is that risk of failure outweighing the potential for success for you?

Don't doubt yourself—at least not until after you've given it a fair shot.

You could be holding on to that solution that's ready to thrust you into the spotlight. Suck it up and say, "I may fail, but if I do at least I will know one way it won't work." Check it off your list, step back, and reevaluate. Look for the new angle and come at it again. Repeat until success. It's that easy.

Come on, you figured out how a man could walk through a wall, for crying out loud! You had it right but just talked yourself out of the answer. You're better than you think you are.

There are honestly no guarantees of success, but there is one surefire guarantee of failure. That answer was given to us by Hall of Famer Wayne Gretzky when he said, "You miss 100% of the shots you don't take."

Step out there and take a shot at it. You just might surprise yourself.

We never truly know what our limitations are until we push ourselves far enough to reach them.

"It's still magic even if you know how it's done." – *Terry Pratchett*

Second Guess

Toward the end, he strode,
Weary but unwilling to stop,
Onward to uncertain victory.
Oftentimes standing alone,
Finding his true friends were few,
He nevertheless would not give in,
Even though failure seemed inevitable.
And as he stood his ground,
Raising his voice in defiance,
The solution appeared before him,
Showing he had made the right choice.

Response Time

What idea do you have right now that you'd love to have the courage to share with someone?

_____

_____

_____

What have you done to help make your idea more likely to succeed?

_____

_____

_____

If you knew you could succeed at anything you put your hand to do, what would field of work would you drop everything to go into?

_____

_____

_____

IT COULDN'T BE DONE...UNTIL IT WAS

"Unlike a mere deception or a simple secret, which gives the impression that something's been taken away, a great magician makes you feel like something's been given to you." – *Jim Steinmeyer*

So which type of spectator are you? Do you seek an answer with such passion that nothing will dissuade you, or do you simply label yourself as average and don't think you're capable of more? Are you willing to fight past the failures to see success or do you just want to quit before even getting started?

My oldest son was never very athletic. One day a few years ago, he came home with his arms loaded down with bags full of healthy food, vitamins, and protein powders. He joined a gym. He started running and working out, all the while watching what he ate.

And he was disciplined. My wife would make brownies, and he would politely refuse one. We would eat fried foods galore while he stuck to his tiny healthy dish.

The end result was he had to buy a whole new wardrobe of smaller clothes.

We took family pictures by the beach the following year, and when they came back, two things about the picture blew me away.

First, the incredible change in my son from previous photographs. When you see someone all the time, gradual changes over time don't always register. That's why you run into someone you graduated high school with and think "Holy cow, when did they get old?", while at the same time seeing yourself in the mirror and thinking you've still got it going on.

When I compared pictures, I realized he had accomplished so much.

Unfortunately, the second thing I saw was how big I looked next to him. At that time in my life, I was dealing with a weight problem myself, and I'd never had the desire to acknowledge or fix it. Suddenly I did.

July 7, 2014, became my "rebirth" day. I joined my son's gym. I bought the foods he bought. I didn't have the drive to be a runner like him, but I hit the weights hard.

Three grueling months later, I had reached my goal and was a middle-aged man in the absolute best shape of his life. And I ended up buying a new smaller wardrobe as well. My son's desire to better himself inspired me to become a different person.

In the midst of our changing, I found a poem that I now have framed in my house. It was my mantra during that time in my life and still inspires me today.

The poem is *"It Couldn't Be Done"* by Edgar Albert Guest.

Somebody said that it couldn't be done
  But he with a chuckle replied
That "maybe it couldn't," but he would be one
  Who wouldn't say so till he'd tried.
So he buckled right in with the trace of a grin
  On his face. If he worried he hid it.
He started to sing as he tackled the thing
  That couldn't be done, and he did it!

Somebody scoffed: "Oh, you'll never do that;
  At least no one ever has done it;"
But he took off his coat and he took off his hat
  And the first thing we knew he'd begun it.
With a lift of his chin and a bit of a grin,
  Without any doubting or quiddit,
He started to sing as he tackled the thing
  That couldn't be done, and he did it.

There are thousands to tell you it cannot be
  done,
  There are thousands to prophesy failure,
There are thousands to point out to you one by
  one,
  The dangers that wait to assail you.
But just buckle in with a bit of a grin,
  Just take off your coat and go to it;
Just start in to sing as you tackle the thing
  That "cannot be done," and you'll do it.

What unachievable thing do you want to accomplish? Maybe it's not a miracle you need to create. Maybe you want to learn a new language, or a musical instrument, or get out of debt, start a new business, or maybe you want to repair some relationship in your life.

So, the question should be: What kind of spectator are you?

- ✓ It can't be done.
- ✓ I wonder how they did it?
- ✓ I wonder how *I* could do it?

Are you willing to throw in the extra effort needed to see it take place?

R.H. Macy had seven unsuccessful businesses before finally launching "Macy's". Stephen King was rejected thirty times before selling *Carrie* for publication. Richard Branson started four-hundred companies before launching Virgin Airlines. Sylvester Stallone was rejected over a thousand times with his script for a movie called "Rocky". James Dyson created over five-thousand prototypes for his vacuum cleaner before succeeding. Thomas Edison is said to have made over ten-thousand prototypes for the light bulb before finding the one that worked.

What do all of those success stories have in common? They refused to give up. They kept on trying and improving on their ideas until the point came where they finally found success.

Just because I've tried to give you the inspiration to push past your normal quit point and continue on to hopefully find success doesn't mean you'll be guaranteed to fix your problem on your next attempt. You may not find a solution with your next five tries. You may have to keep circling that problem and trying to look at it from all angles for a while before you finally find a way to solve it.

> *Don't give up until you find the solution. That's the biggest secret to success anyone could ever give you.*

But don't give up. Don't quit. Don't stop.

I heard a story about a man who got lost in the

woods for several weeks without food or supplies. He kept walking, trying to find his way back to civilization but didn't see anyone. After climbing several mountains and tall hills, he found himself at the bottom of yet another steep hill but apparently couldn't find the strength to push through. His body was found at the foot of that steep hill, while on the other side of it was a campground filled with vacationers. He was just one more climb away from rescue.

Napoleon Hill said, "When temporary defeat overtakes a man, the easiest and most logical thing to do is to quit. That is exactly what the majority of men do. More than five hundred of the most successful men this country has ever known said their greatest success came just one step beyond the point at which temporary defeat had overtaken them."

Don't give up until you find the solution. That's the biggest secret to success anyone could ever give you.

Don't ever isolate yourself or think your problem is too unique for anyone to help you with it. The odds are someone somewhere has faced something similar and found a way through. Even if they haven't, the things they have tried and failed with can show you steps you can avoid or approach differently.

Be the leader you would want to follow.

Keep an open mind, look at what others have done in the past to accomplish your goal, and then take a look at yourself—your gifts, abilities, and knowledge. Think "It *can* be done. How can *I* make it happen?".

At *that moment*, you will have taken the first real step toward becoming a magician.

<u>Response Time</u>

Look at your own "impossible thing" you listed from the first chapter's response time. Does it still seem so impossible?

_____

_____

_____

What idea have you given up on in the past that is worth revisiting at this place in your life?

_____

_____

_____

_____

Who has inspired you in the past? What have you done to let them know they made a difference?

_____

_____

_____

_____

"And above all watch with glittering eyes the whole world around you because the greatest secrets are always hidden in the most unlikely of places. Those who don't believe in magic will never find it."
- *Roald Dahl*

"If we believe in magic, we'll live a magical life."
- *Tony Robbins*

THE MIRACULOUS ANSWER

"The most important thing in life is to stop saying I wish and start saying I will. Consider nothing impossible, then treat possibilities as probabilities." – *David Copperfield*

Occasionally I perform shows for children, and I have found it to be a wildly unpredictable experience. Sometimes I am a wizard of unimaginable power to them, while other times I am a trickster who has come to fool them and therefore I must be exposed right there in the middle of my show. All these children watching the same show experience it very differently.

There is this sad period in our lives that we may not even realize happens. I call it "The Years of Lost Magic".

For a child up until the age of about 9, there is this unending sense of belief and wonder. They believe in magic, and they believe that rabbit really did come from the hat, or the rope really did get cut and put back together again.

Around 14 or 15, we develop that sense again, in a more mature way. We don't necessarily believe in real magic, but we have an appreciation for the unexplainable things we see the magician do. We *want* to believe in magic, and sometimes that is enough.

But in that little window of ages 9-13, the desire to believe in wonder is replaced by the desperate need for clear-cut answers. They are the "truthers". "How did that cut rope get restored? Maybe he didn't cut it at all, or maybe it was two ropes and he switched them, or maybe he's just hiding something in his hand. Never mind what he just did or how cool it looked, tell us how it was done!"

The sad truth is that kids that age can often miss the moment simply because their focus is on the explanation behind it. Nothing less than the whole truth will suffice.

It never ceases to shock me at how a room full of children of various ages can experience completely different moments in the same show. For smaller kids, it was amazing and fun. For older kids and adults, it was mysterious and exciting. But for the "truthers", it was no big deal because they know how it all was done. They are just as cool as the magician because they think they know his secrets (even though they usually don't).

And here we are at the end of this trip with you. Where will you fit in now that you have seen behind the curtain?

You have the tools. You have the mindset. And you might be thinking "That's too easy...it'll never work."

But it will if applied correctly.

Don't overthink it. Don't toss it away because I didn't teach you some magic word that allowed you to instantly bend reality around you (JK Rowling actually did that in one of the Harry Potter books, but no one seems to have caught it yet).

Develop that mentality of wonder. Don't allow yourself to give up too soon.

And there's one more thing I'd like to point out about magic through the various age ranges.

Somewhere around fifty years old, that childlike desire for pure magic starts to return. Maybe it's because we've spent so much of our lives jaded and desperately want some nostalgic comfort of our youth. Maybe it's just because reality sucks and we need to believe there is more to life than just what we are experiencing day to day.

Whatever it is, it is a beautiful thing to see.

Card tricks fascinate us again. Coins appear and disappear right before our eyes and we gasp in amazement. Reality shifts just a little, and we are in a new feeling and experience.

We believe because we *want* to believe. We

suspend our disbelief because we *need* the miraculous in our lives. We hold out hope that there truly *is* magic in the world somehow.

We stop caring how it's all done and instead enjoy the moment.

This phenomena is something I have discovered throughout my performances. I can't tell you how many times I've done a trick for someone in that age range and they say, "How did you do that? Wait, don't tell me. I don't want to know."

They simply want to hold on to that magic.

> *Develop that mentality of wonder. Don't allow yourself to give up too soon.*

In the next chapter, I will tell you about the moment that same thing happened in my own life recently, but for now, let's bring it all back around to you and your "impossible" problem.

Think back to the magic trick I described in the third chapter when introducing the three types of spectators: the spectator is sitting on a card throughout an entire trick, and it's their signed card.

Let's throw my three-step process into the mix and make this happen. **First, I have to approach it with an open mind. It can be done when I find the answer.**

A person cannot be sitting on a card they haven't even signed yet in the real world. If I just accept that and walk away, the trick is dead before it ever began. I have to say it *can* be done.

Second, I have to look at what others have done in the past to achieve a similar goal.

Believe it or not, the trick has been done in some form or fashion before. I have no less than five different versions of the trick in various magic books I own. Five is a manageable number, so I read all of them to find suggestions.

On the other hand, if I found thirty different versions, I could get stuck in "research mode" and never do anything. In that case, I would choose the top five or six closest to what I am trying to accomplish and go from there.

Third, I have to ask how I am uniquely gifted to solve this problem? What quirks, ideas, and inspirations can I bring to solving the equation?

I know what I want to accomplish with the trick, I have researched various ways others have done something similar in the past, and here we are at the big moment: will I make this my own or stay a copy of others?

Instead, I found my own particular handling of how to accomplish the trick. It suits my personality. The way I perform it is unique, though I acknowledge that I was influenced by previous magicians and what they had done before.

Those are the methods in action by a magician to create a trick. I told you it worked for us.

I have given you three steps toward finding a solution to whatever problem you are trying to tackle. I have told you time and again to "ignore the impossible".

I have not given you the answer to your problem, but there *is* one person who most likely has the answer to the problem you are facing.

You.

Find the miraculous answer you are holding in.

You're probably thinking, "What kind of suggestion is that? I came *here* for the miraculous answer. Why on earth would I be holding it in?"

But I'm serious. Somewhere out there is the answer to your problem. I'm willing to bet *you* are the miracle-worker you need to answer it.

You. Not someone else.

You have the potential to be miraculous.

Think about that "impossible" problem in your life. You probably think it would take a miracle to solve it right now. If you were to come up with the answer tomorrow, you'd think it was a miracle.

You would be a miracle-worker.

You would be miraculous. So, stop fooling

yourself and waiting for someone else to fix it all.

Someone is going to come up with the answer to your problem. Why can't it be you?

Now the question is do you have the drive to be that miracle worker? And I know I've said this before, but is it really "impossible"?

I don't think we always need a miracle (though we do from time to time, amen?). I've told you before in this book that I believe sometimes we only need to change our viewpoint, rethink things, and approach them differently. We give up too easily.

You probably already have the answer bouncing around in your head desperately trying to get out.

Just look at what you did in these few pages.

> ➢ You found a way to write an entire string of random letters from memory after just a few seconds when your first thought was that it would take you much longer.
> ➢ You figured out how it would be possible

to walk through a brick wall on a stage surrounded by spectators. You may have driven yourself to doubt in the end, but at one point you had it.

You have already solved two "impossible" challenges!

Now accept the fact that the miraculous answer to your impossible problem just might be in you.

Activate that belief in yourself.

I have talked to so many people in my life that came from bad backgrounds. Things were said over them as they were growing up that should never have been spoken. Limitations were put on them by other people who didn't know what they were truly capable of achieving. And in the end, those self-imposed limitations robbed the world of much-needed beauty.

Think of how many books have never been written because the author didn't think they were good enough and never took the time to sit down and write. Their success story might have even eclipsed the stories of Stephen King and JK Rowling, but they gave up instead.

Imagine how many beautiful paintings will never be seen because the artist doubted themselves into inaction.

Consider how many amazing songs will never be heard because the musician or songwriter just didn't think they had it in them and lived their life playing other peoples' music.

How many teams will lose some important game because the person who was supposed to be their star player gave up on the sport the first time they failed?

Remember Walt Disney's story from an earlier chapter? He was fired from a newspaper job specifically because he "lacked imagination and had no good ideas". He could have pictured himself as a failure and just spent his life doing average things with average people. Instead, he refused to let those words destroy him. And now we can honestly say the world is forever changed because of his determination. If you don't believe me, look at any children around you. Chances are good they are wearing some cartoon character on their clothes that Disney helped inspire in some fashion.

Disney said, "Get a good idea, and stay with it; dog it, and work at it until it's done and done right."

What are you robbing the world of today?

You may think, "Well, I'm not an artist, author, athlete, or songwriter and I have no desire to be." That may be true, but what about the things you *are* interested in and are good at? Have you given up on them too soon?

Have you allowed yourself to wallow in doubt and second-guessing simply because you gave up on your passion and belief in yourself years ago?

Think about it this: Who understands your problem better than you? Probably no one.

Who has the intricate knowledge needed to understand all sides of the situation? Most likely it's you.

Who is best qualified to solve the problem? Maybe you feel like it's somebody else, but it's in your hands, and it's up to you. Prove the naysayers wrong.

Now, what more do you need to find that answer?

Do you need more input? Gather your team and brainstorm. If you don't have a team, build one.

> "There are two types of people who will tell you that you cannot make a difference in this world: those who are afraid to try and those who are afraid you will succeed." –
> Ray Goforth

Do you need more details? Research every aspect of it and be fearless in your determination to examine it from all sides.

Do you need more options? Start making lists and don't make them all pessimist. Create lists that have positive outlooks on some decisions if there are any. And in your brainstorm sessions don't allow any possibility to be immediately tossed out. Even if something isn't a correct answer, it might possibly spark some creative idea in another direction later.

Whatever you need, fearlessly strive to achieve it. Activate that belief in yourself that may lie dormant in your core.

Light the creative spark inside you that can lead you to the answer—the miraculous possibilities in yourself.

Nothing is guaranteed, and nothing is sure-fire, but should you stop trying simply because it's too hard?

I read a quote that has been attributed to a number of people over the years:

> *"Watch your thoughts, they become words;*
> *watch your words, they become actions;*
> *watch your actions, they become habits;*
> *watch your habits, they become character;*
> *watch your character, for it becomes your*
> *destiny."*

It definitely seems to be the case in a lot of examples, and I believe you could probably live by those rules and succeed. However, I like this example a little more. Just remember the word

"WATCH".

W – Watch your **W**ords

A – Watch your **A**ctions

T – Watch your **T**houghts

C – Watch your **C**haracter

H – Watch your **H**abits

The things you believe about yourself can influence your success or failure more than anything else. Even if the world thinks you're crazy, if you believe you're right, you are more likely to find a way to succeed.

But on the flip side, if we allow ourselves to entertain the *probability* of failure in an endeavor, we are often creating a self-fulfilling prophecy against our success.

Be brave and start speaking positive things over your life. Let your thoughts create powerful words that will motivate you to action that becomes a habit that can forever change your character for good.

To get a little more casual with it, the old phrase "haters gonna hate" comes to mind. There are those who will never believe in you or your ideas. You will have to be strong enough to keep at it until you succeed.

Ray Goforth said, "There are two types of people who will tell you that you cannot make a difference in this world: those who are afraid to try and those who are afraid you will succeed."

I know it may sound a little crazy and "out there", but it works. Positive words can create positive actions in your life.

Don't be afraid to believe in yourself.

Thomas Edison once said, "Our greatest weakness lies in giving up. The most certain way to succeed is always to try just one more time."

Go hit that "impossible" problem one more time. And again, if need be. Keep going until you solve it.

Because you can.

Response Time

What is one thing you wish you'd done earlier in your life, or what is the one thing you think you gave up on too soon?

_____

_____

_____

What is one option you have not yet considered in solving your "impossible" problem because it seemed too far-fetched? Could it possibly be tweaked to begin to work or at least help solve the problem?

_____

_____

_____

What has someone spoken over you in the past that you have mistakenly allowed yourself to believe and/or adapt as truth—even though it's not?

_____

_____

_____

FINAL THOUGHTS

"To those who believe, no explanation is necessary. To those who do not, no explanation will suffice." – *Joseph Dunninger*

I know that I have harped on it a lot throughout the book, but do you see now how your seemingly "impossible problem" really isn't necessarily so overwhelming?

When you go to Universal Studios in Orlando, you can see various movie sets created throughout the park. The surprising detail about many of them is that they are facades. Once you get around the corner of some building, you find that it was only the front of the structure with nothing behind it to support it. It looks huge on one side but is pretty unimpressive from the other. The thing that seemed overwhelming at first really isn't once you see it from other angles.

Hopefully, that's the way you are looking at your problem now; you aren't still standing there staring at it but have started truly examining all aspects of the situation to break them down to a manageable state.

In case you haven't figured it out yet, my entire purpose in this book has been to get you to remove the word "impossible" from your vocabulary when dealing with problem-solving. My ulterior motive in everything I said was to help you develop the confidence in yourself to run *to* the battle rather than wave the flag of surrender before you gave it the first try.

I have a feeling there will be some of you out there who might feel a little discouraged at this point as we reach the end of the book. Maybe you still haven't found that answer even after having shared this journey with me. I didn't give you the answer; I merely pointed you in the direction of how to find it.

But now that you know the methods, you have opened the door to the one last secret I want to share about magic in this book.

There is technically a *fourth* type of spectator that magicians perform for: other magicians.

That may not sound like such a big deal, and it may even seem like they should fit into one of those other categories, yet they don't. The reason is simple yet sad in a way: we know how it's done. We have peeked behind the curtain and seen the wizard.

I don't know exactly when—maybe it's the fiftieth card trick you learn or the one-hundredth you see—but for whatever reason it happens.

We lose the sense of wonder.

We see a card trick and are impressed by the technical skill needed to pull it off, but we have a general idea of what was required to make that work. There is no magic in it.

I don't think that happens with doctors. I don't know any doctors well enough to ask them the tough questions, but I can't believe they'd watch another doctor perform some delicate brain surgery and think, "Pfffft, big deal. I could do that."

I know how most tricks are done. Maybe not the exact method that particular magician used at the time, but I know enough to be able to perform a version of most tricks I see. I'm not bragging; I'm just saying I've studied a lot and been to a lot of conventions and lectures to learn as much as I could.

However, there was one magician who was able to instill in me that feeling of being a spectator again for the first time with no clue as to how the magic was happening. His name was Eugene Burger.

You can watch Eugene perform on various YouTube clips out there (and I encourage you to). He was this smiling, unassuming little man who always wore black and had a flowing gray beard that would have made Gandalf jealous. He had a booming voice and a gregarious laugh that immediately drew you into his orbit. He was one of the best magicians I'd ever seen, yet his fame is almost completely unknown to anyone besides other magicians.

And one day, Eugene did the impossible for me: he made me believe in magic again.

In 2015, My sons and I were at The Winter Carnival of Magic, a magic convention in Pigeon Forge, Tennessee (if you are seriously interested in magic, it's a great convention to go to). I had spent a few days surrounded by incredible magicians who presented some wonderful illusions. At the end of the convention, there was a big pizza party in a hotel lobby, and the three of us were sitting at a table eating pizza while just watching other folks around us.

From out of nowhere, Eugene plopped into the empty seat at our table and said, "Would you guys like to see some magic?". We were astonished to see one of our favorite magicians of the conference suddenly sitting with us, so we all stuttered a definite yes.

For the next few minutes, Eugene performed card tricks for us. I was sitting just a foot away from him, my eyes glued to the cards, and I never caught a single move. Quite simply, he worked miracles with the pasteboards that night.

When he had finished showing us his magic, he smiled, thanked us for our attention, and started to get up. I quickly asked him if those tricks were in print somewhere. He winked and said, "Those are ones I save for me. But they'll be published after I'm dead in a book called *Eugene Burger from the Grave.*"

I thought he was joking. He wasn't. Eugene passed away in 2017, and true to his word there are two books of his waiting to be published with those miracles in them. I will definitely buy them because I own all of his books, but I don't know if I will ever read them. He instilled in me a sense of wonder I hadn't even realized I'd lost. I cherish those moments too much to spoil them by looking behind the curtain again.

And now you have been given the opportunity to glimpse the truth about a magician's way of thinking. You may have unconsciously moved to that fourth type of spectator now, no matter which of the first three you initially were.

But please don't. Don't allow this knowledge to go to waste unused in your situation. Don't become jaded and lose that sense of possibilities in your life.

You need to understand that magic tricks are rarely as difficult as you would imagine. When I perform a trick, people give me all sorts of explanations that are incredibly intricate and involve much more time and effort than I would be willing to give. Honestly, it's usually something as simple as making you believe you saw something you didn't actually see. It's "misdirection", remember?

When I teach a magic trick to someone, they inevitably issue a disappointed little "Really?" and then tell me how much harder they had made it in their head. It's just like the "Houdini and the wall" situation from the first chapter.

Likewise, many of our problems are rarely as difficult as we make them out to be. They may seem insurmountable at first glance, but how about at that second or third glance?

Don't throw the things I've discussed in this book away as "too simple". You have been exposed to the process of creating a miracle from a magician's point of view, and that roundabout creativity can influence your way of thinking when it comes to tackling your problems—if you apply it and do it.

> *Many of our problems may seem insurmountable at first glance, but how about at that second or third glance?*

Like that famous Jedi master Yoda said, "Do or do not. There is no 'try'."

Make it happen in your life. Stop beating your head against a wall using old tactics that may have worked in the past but just aren't working now. Give them a shot, and then use them to springboard your thinking into new and varied avenues.

I don't know what you were expecting as we began, but these truly are the steps I use to create an illusion.

I didn't read you anything from some ancient mystic scrolls of wisdom. I just gave you three steps for problem-solving and hopefully shined a light on the type of spectator you never realized you were. In the process, I hope you've discovered a challenge to grow in your thinking.

Just because something is simple doesn't make it without merit. It's not rocket science to tie your shoes...but skip it for a day and see how important it can be.

Thank you for taking this journey with me. I hope it's been entertaining for you, and it's my sincere wish that something you've read inspires you to create your own form of magic in your life and situations.

Now it's time to teach you how to perform a magic trick...

"We don't need magic to transform the world. We carry all the power we need inside ourselves already. "
– *JK Rowling*

"The magic is inside you. There ain't no crystal ball." – *Dolly Parton*

If you do apply the principles I've laid out here and found a solution to an "impossible" problem in your life, please take a second to email me (**Brian@BrianReaves.net**) and let me know.

I will be updating my website with *your* success stories.

IgnoreTheImpossible.com

If you would like to watch Brian's TEDxBirmingham presentation of "Ignore the Impossible", you can view it at this link:

http://www.BrianReaves.net/motivational-speaking

Or scan this code:

TIME TO LEARN A MAGIC TRICK!

"The art of a magician is to create wonder. If we live with a sense of wonder, our lives become filled with joy."
  – Doug Hennig

"The real secret of magic lies in the performance."
  -David Copperfield

Here is the trick I promised to teach you. I have chosen something you should be able to do with nothing more than office supplies you might have at hand. Practice this, learn the script, and get out there to amaze your co-workers.

But be warned: the first time you experience what it's like to share the magic with someone, you may find yourself headed on a late-night trip to the bookstore to learn more. Don't say I didn't warn you.

THE EFFECT: The magician shows a spectator three different colored markers and a piece of paper. As he turns his back, he instructs them to pick a color and sign their name. After they have done so, they are told to put the paper in their pocket and mix up the pens so there's no way to know what color has been used.

When they are finished, the magician turns around and after a few seconds is able to tell the spectator exactly which color they chose.

This trick can be done to two spectators at once (or more if you are feeling particularly magical).

MATERIALS NEEDED: Three different colored Sharpie markers and a piece of paper.

SETUP: Take the caps off your Sharpie and position them so the clip lines up with the "Sharpie" logo on the pen.

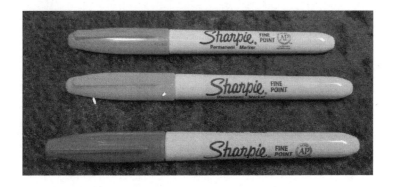

Now bring in your spectators.

THE ROUTINE: Gather a few folks together and have one be your spectator.

Say: "I don't know if you've heard this or not, but a person makes a lot of subconscious choices throughout the day based on their personality type. With your help, I'd like to demonstrate what I mean.

"I'm going to turn my back in a minute. When I do, please take one of the markers—whichever color you feel drawn to—and sign your name on the paper. Then put the paper in your pocket, put the top back on the marker, and mix them all up so I can't possibly know which one you've chosen."

After they do so, you turn around and glance down at the markers. One of them should be different from the other two with the clip not exactly right on the logo.

That's the one they chose.

Do this quickly. Don't spend a lot of time studying the markers or you'll give it away. It should be nothing more than you glancing down and noticing the markers are mixed up as you asked.

Now look them in the eyes and appear to study them carefully for a moment.

Say: "A lot of people make obvious choices, but I think you tried to throw me off. I believe you had one color marker in mind but you deliberately chose another because you thought I'd say that first. As a matter of fact, I think you chose _____ (whatever color they chose)."

Have them pull out the paper with their name on it to confirm you were correct and accept your gracious applause.

What if it doesn't work? What if they put the marker cap back on right and you can't tell which one they used?

In that case, study them for a moment and say, "I think I know which one you chose. Let's make this a little bit more of a challenge by getting someone else to help."

Pick another spectator. "I'm going to turn my back again, and I'd like you to choose a *different* color from the one they did and sign your name as well."

After they say they have done so, you should be able to turn around and see a marker mixed up this time. Since you told them to choose a different color from the one chosen by the first spectator, you know which color the second spectator chose.

You can correctly guess the second spectator's choice, and you have a 50/50 guess on the first one. If you miss the first, you still have gotten the second one.

If you are having trouble seeing which pen was chosen, you can pick each one up individually and point it at the spectator like a magic wand. This gives you a chance to study the pen a little more closely, but don't just stare at the pen. Talk while you are waving it as if trying to read some psychic signals off of it or their energy signature.

If you are brave, you can do this for two people at the same time. Just have the first spectator make their choice. When you turn around and see which one they chose, tell the second spectator to choose a *different* color and do the same. When you turn back around, you'll see the second marker that's mixed up and know exactly who chose what.

As I told you before, once you know the secret to a trick it doesn't seem as impressive, but this trick works if done correctly. Just make sure you set the markers up *before* you call for your spectators. Maybe you can have them casually sitting on your desk when they arrive, and then you say, "Let me show you something I read in a magic book..."

This trick can be done with any pen that has a logo on it and a removable top with a clip, so if all you have are a few different colored ballpoint pens around, you can still perform this. Just make sure the color difference will be easy for you to spot as you turn around.

Magic is all about practice and presentation. Practice the trick by yourself until you can see which pen was touched with nothing more than a glance. When you finally present it to someone, don't rush things. Take your time and enjoy every minute of it. Make it seem like you're actually trying to read their mind. Be mysterious. Have fun with it!

Perhaps the most important thing to remember is what you've read about the three types of spectators in this book. After the effect is over, listen to their reaction and try to gauge for yourself into which category they fall.

If you enjoyed this example and would like to learn more magic that's fun and easy to do, I would suggest *The Magic Book* by Harry Lorayne.

ABOUT THE AUTHOR

Brian Reaves is an award-winning illusionist and author. He has been voted Birmingham's "Magician of the Year" three times by his peers in the International Brotherhood of Magicians and was the Close-Up Champion of the Winter Carnival of Magic in 2016. In 2017, Brian was the opening speaker at TEDx Birmingham with his "Ignore the Impossible" speech.

With over 25 years' experience both in the art of magic and in corporate training, Brian has crafted a unique method to present his message using illusions to illustrate points in the presentation and make it a memorable, interactive experience for all who attend.

He and his wife live in a comic book museum near Birmingham, Alabama.

Before you go...

Please note that **the following page won't mean much to you right now**. Don't turn the page! If you do come to one of my talks or shows, bring this book with you and I'll work a miracle with a deck of cards for you.

By the way, there are two other magic tricks in this book you most likely didn't notice. Again, bring this book to a talk or one of my shows, and you might be amazed at what you've missed.

So skip this last page and let's have some fun next time we get together.

Thanks for reading. If you have any questions or comments, I'd love to hear them. Email me at **Brian@BrianReaves.net** and let's chat!

Ignore the Impossible

My apologies for not being able to find your three of spades.

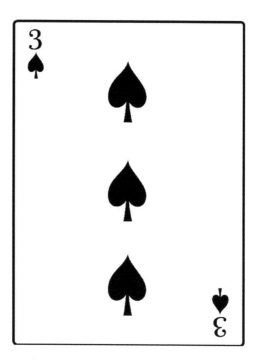

Made in the USA
Middletown, DE
18 July 2023